Understanding the Elements of the Periodic Table™

ARSENIC

Greg Roza

33

75

As

rosen publishing's
rosen central®

New York

For Cindy

Published in 2009 by The Rosen Publishing Group, Inc.
29 East 21st Street, New York, NY 10010
www.rosenpublishing.com

First Edition

Library of Congress Cataloging-in-Publication Data

Roza, Greg.
Arsenic / Greg Roza.
        p. cm.—(Understanding the elements of the periodic table)
Includes bibliographical references and index.
ISBN-13: 978-1-4042-1782-9 (library binding)
1. Arsenic—Juvenile literature. 2. Chemical elements—Juvenile literature.
I. Title.
QD181.A7R69 2009
546'.715—dc22

                                                                    2007041768

Manufactured in Malaysia

On the cover: Arsenic's square on the periodic table of elements. Inset: The atomic structure of arsenic.

Contents

Introduction

Arsenic (chemical symbol: As) was widely known as a deadly poison for many centuries, especially among the wealthy and royalty. The earliest record of arsenic's deadly power comes from the first century CE writings of the Greek physician Dioscorides. However, it had been used for evil purposes since the fourth century BCE. At that time, the Romans frequently used arsenic for political gain. Many Roman women reportedly used arsenic to kill men so they would profit from their deaths. Purposeful arsenic poisoning became so common that, in 82 BCE, the Roman dictator Lucius Cornelius Sulla issued a law against poisoning.

Arsenic was a murder weapon widely used, particularly by women, during the Renaissance and the Victorian Age. It was easy for women to poison people because they were often expected to cook food and administer medicines. Poisons such as arsenic were also easy to obtain because they were used to kill rats and other pests. Arsenic was even used in makeup! It was also easy to hide arsenic poisoning because its effects resemble illnesses that were widespread during these eras.

Perhaps the most famous arsenic murder story involves Pope Alexander VI, his son Cesare, and his daughter Lucrezia Borgia. Alexander became pope in 1492. During his reign, Lucrezia sequentially married several influential politicians and nobles to empower Pope Alexander's family and strengthen his control of Italy. Rumor says that when Lucrezia's husbands

Arsenic was once stored in ceramic containers like the one shown here. Notice the word "arsenic" is followed by a well-known symbol for poison—a skull and crossbones.

no longer proved valuable to the pope, he had them murdered—often by poisoning. Lucrezia may or may not have had a role in these murders. Some legends say that she owned a ring with a hidden compartment filled with arsenic. She would secretly pour the poison into a victim's wine. Today, Lucrezia is often remembered as a ruthless woman who married and murdered the men who stood in the way of her father's advancement.

King of Poisons

Although much of Lucrezia's story may be the product of legend, arsenic has long played a major role as a poison in fact as well as fiction. Over the years, it has become known as the Poison of Kings, and the King of Poisons. The French tyrant Napoléon Bonaparte (1769–1821) died of arsenic poisoning. For years, people assumed his death by arsenic poisoning was the result of murder. However, other historians and chemists think the arsenic came from the wallpaper in the room where he died, which contained a popular green pigment made from arsenic called Scheele's green. Scientists have proven that microorganisms in wallpaper paste turned the arsenic in Scheele's green into a vapor. Napoléon probably

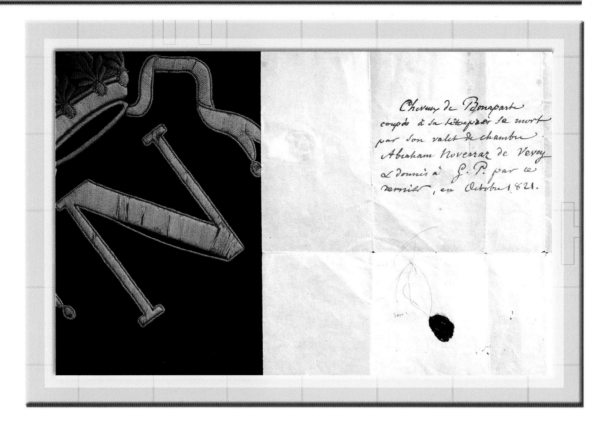

A sample of Napoléon's hair has been sealed to a certificate of authenticity. French scientists examined the hair in 2001 and found that it contained an amount of arsenic seven to thirty-eight times higher than normal.

breathed in the arsenic for weeks before his death. Whether this is what killed him or not is still under discussion.

Today, arsenic poisoning has become an issue in many areas of modern life. Arsenic has useful and important applications in our world, including in the manufacture of medicines, pesticides, electrical circuitry, and glass. Even though arsenic is not used as much as it once was, educating the public about its dangers has helped reduce accidental poisonings and increased arsenic's value in our society.

Chapter One
The History of Arsenic

In 1991, in the Alps on the border between Austria and Italy, two hikers came across the body of a man who had died and had been frozen in ice for about 5,300 years! Scientists discovered an abnormally high amount of arsenic in the man's hair. This led some to believe that the man once worked with metals, specifically copper (Cu). Arsenic is a common contaminant of copper. When refining copper from copper ores, ancient metalworkers often inhaled arsenic vapors that were released during the heating process. This would explain why the iceman had such high levels of arsenic in his hair. We now know that people have been affected by arsenic poisoning for at least 5,300 years.

The Ancient History of Arsenic

Arsenic, in the form of its compounds, was one of the earliest elements to be used by humans. Ores that contained both copper and arsenic were known as early as 3600 BCE. Scientists have found evidence of the use of arsenic in the ancient cultures of China, Greece, Persia, and Egypt. The Greeks called the element arsenicon. This was derived from the Persian word *az-zarnikh*, which means "yellow orpiment" (orpiment is a mineral that contains arsenic).

Oetzi—who was named after the Oetzi Valley, where he was found—is the oldest natural mummy discovered in Europe. Research on his hair showed that it had high levels of arsenic and copper, which might mean that Oetzi had worked with copper.

Throughout the Bronze Age (c. 3500–1100 BCE), arsenic was mixed with bronze to make it stronger. To make bronze, copper ore—which often contains small amounts of arsenic—is melted with tin (Sn) and sometimes other elements. Bronze made with

Who Was Albertus Magnus?

Albertus Magnus (1206?–1280), also known as Saint Albert the Great, was a Dominican friar who first isolated pure arsenic. During his life, Albertus was a well-known Christian theologian, philosopher, and scientist. He is remembered for his assertion that religion and science are different but equally meaningful systems of thought. He believed that different areas of thought—particularly religion and science—followed distinct sets of laws. He was one of the most influential German philosophers of the Middle Ages. He also wrote extensively on many subjects, including astronomy, chemistry, mineralogy, music, philosophy, logic, botany, and alchemy. Albertus was canonized by Pope Pius XI in 1931. He was also officially named a Doctor of the Church. His feast day is celebrated on November 15.

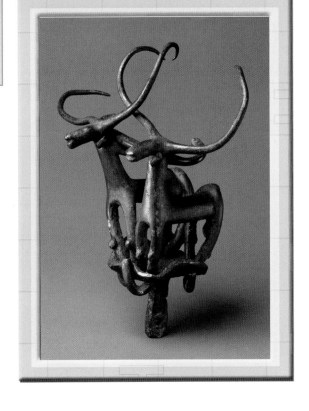

This sculpture of two long-horned bulls, made in Turkey between 2400 and 2000 BCE, is composed of arsenical copper.

arsenic, called arsenical bronze, is stronger than regular bronze. Inhaling the arsenic vapors produced when it is heated, however, often caused metalworkers to have health problems later in life.

Isolating Arsenic

Minerals containing arsenic, particularly arsenopyrite, orpiment, and realgar, were widely used prior to the Middle Ages. Most historians believe pure arsenic was first isolated by German theologian, philosopher, and scientist Albertus Magnus in 1250. Arsenic was the first element to be isolated since ancient times. It is also the earliest isolated element whose discoverer is known. Albertus isolated arsenic by heating the mineral orpiment (arsenic sulfide) with soap.

Arsenic in the Victorian Age

During the Victorian Age, in the mid- to late 1800s, arsenic played a strange role in people's lives. Many products contained arsenic pigments, including wallpaper, paints, and fabrics. Scheele's green pigment could be found in a majority of homes. People were poisoned by breathing it in for extended periods of time. It had become known that small doses of arsenic solutions could act as stimulants. One medication, which became known as "Fowler's

Albertus Magnus is shown here as a scholar in a fourteenth-century fresco by Italian artist Tommaso da Modena. Albertus Magnus is considered by historians to be the first person to have isolated pure arsenic.

solution," contained potassium arsenite. It was prescribed throughout the nineteenth century and well into the twentieth century as a remedy for many problems, including malaria and asthma.

Arsenic was sometimes used by Victorian women to make their skin whiter. Pale skin was a sign that a person did not have to do physical labor, and many thought it made them appear more feminine. Most women easily obtained arsenic from their local pharmacists. Arsenic poisoning also became a "trendy" form of murder because so many upper-class women obtained it with relative ease. It became such a popular form of murder that the Arsenic Act was introduced in England in 1851. It stated that arsenic could not be sold to anyone under the age of twenty-one or anyone the pharmacist did not know. Purchasers and the pharmacists had to sign a "poison book" every time the poison was sold. Furthermore, the law required that the poison be mixed with a coloring agent, which made it more difficult to conceal when it was added to a person's food or drink.

The Marsh Test

Arsenic remained a popular choice as a poison for centuries. Over this time, the effects of arsenic poisoning remained unidentified. The symptoms resembled those of cholera, so investigators untrained in the use of arsenic were often fooled by these symptoms.

In the 1830s, an English chemist named James Marsh tried to prove a man used arsenic to murder his grandfather. Marsh used a test recently developed that involved mixing hydrochloric acid and hydrogen sulfide with the contents of the victim's stomach. The result was a yellow solid containing arsenic—if arsenic was in fact present in the victim's stomach. The evidence, however, deteriorated before it could be used in court, and the suspect was released. The outcome bothered Marsh, and he spent the next few years perfecting a new test for arsenic. This test is now known as the Marsh test.

To detect arsenic using the Marsh test, a sample believed to contain the substance is placed in a glass container along with zinc (Zn) and sulfuric acid (H_2SO_4). If the sample contains arsenic, arsine gas (AsH_3) is produced. When the arsine gas is heated in a glass tube, the arsine decomposes and forms pure arsenic, which deposits on the glass. The arsenic deposit on the glass looks like a mirror. The introduction of the Marsh test led to a decline in the number of deliberate arsenic poisonings.

Arsenic in the Modern World

Arsenic compounds have been used for many purposes since the beginning of the nineteenth century. Unfortunately, most of them have resulted in harmful effects to people and the environment. The U.S. government considered using arsenic compounds as poisons in weapons during World War I (1914–1917) and World War II (1939–1945), but other toxic chemicals were used instead. Arsenic-based pesticides are often successful in destroying pests, but they also contaminate the soil and can make people sick. Early versions of pressure-treated lumber used arsenic compounds to preserve the wood, but these compounds could also cause illness in people and animals. Some medications use arsenic, but these, too, are dangerous and must be used carefully. In many areas of life, chemicals that contain arsenic have been replaced by other, less harmful chemicals.

Chapter Two
Arsenic and the Periodic Table

All matter in the universe is made up of very tiny pieces called atoms. They are the smallest pieces of matter that can exist by themselves. Atoms bond with other atoms to form larger pieces of matter called molecules. Some matter, like pure arsenic, is made up of just one type of atom. This type of matter is called an element. Other types of matter are made up of two or more kinds of atoms.

You might be surprised to learn that atoms are made up of even smaller pieces called subatomic particles. The kind and number of subatomic particles in a single atom define what type of matter it is. There are three kinds of subatomic particles. Protons have a positive electrical charge. Neutrons do not have a charge. Protons and neutrons cluster together at the center of the atom, forming the nucleus. Therefore, protons and neutrons are sometimes called nucleons.

Electrons, which are much smaller than protons and neutrons, orbit the nucleus. Electrons have a negative electrical charge. This negative charge is attracted to the

This is a sample of pure arsenic. Arsenic is most often gray, but it develops a black tarnish when exposed to the air.

positive charge of protons. Most of the time this attraction keeps them from flying away from the nucleus. Electrons sometimes leave an atom to join another atom. When this happens, an atom will have an overall positive charge (due to an excess of protons). The atom that receives the electrons will have an overall negative charge (due to an excess of electrons). An atom with a positive or negative charge is called an ion.

Electrons orbit the nucleus in shells, or energy levels. Atoms can have up to seven shells, depending on the number of electrons orbiting the nucleus. A shell may contain a single electron, or it may contain dozens. The shell closest to the nucleus never has more than two electrons. The outermost shell is called the valence shell. The electrons in this shell are

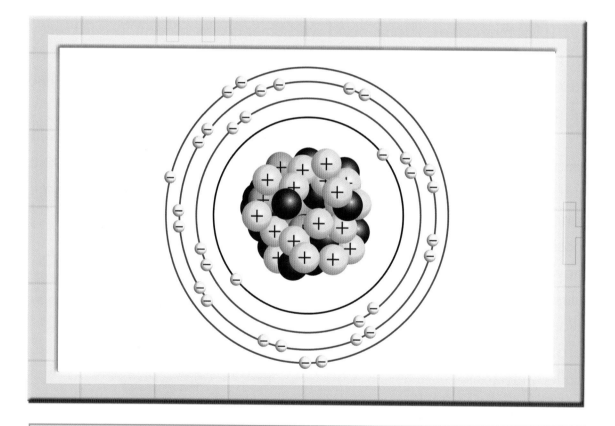

The diagram shown here is an artist's representation of an atom of arsenic. The black particles represent neutrons, and the white particles with plus signs are protons. The smaller white particles with minus signs represent electrons. Arsenic has four energy levels, or shells.

capable of forming bonds between the atom and other atoms. An arsenic atom has thirty-three protons, forty-two neutrons, and thirty-three electrons. It has four electron shells, with five electrons in the valence shell.

Atomic Number and Atomic Weight

The periodic table we use today organizes the elements by the number of protons found in the nucleus of a single atom of each element. (See the periodic table of elements on pages 40–41.) This number is called the atomic number. Hydrogen (H), the first element on the periodic table, has a single proton, so its atomic number is one. Next comes helium (He) with two protons, lithium (Li) with three protons, and so on. Arsenic has thirty-three protons. Therefore, its atomic number is 33.

Dmitry Mendeleyev and the Periodic Table

By the mid-1800s, several systems of organizing the elements had been developed, but no single system was foremost. The Russian chemist Dmitry Mendeleyev was one of the first to develop the periodic table of elements. In 1869, when he listed the elements in order based on their atomic weights (expressed as atomic mass units, or amu), he made an important discovery. Elements with similar properties occurred at regular intervals in the list. He lined up the elements in several rows and arranged the rows so that elements with similar properties were placed in columns. Mendeleyev also included gaps in his table if he didn't know of an element with the properties needed to fill the gap. He predicted the properties of the elements that would fill these gaps. His predictions have been proven true over the years.

33   75

As

The chemical symbol for arsenic is As. The number on the left is its atomic number, 33. The number on the right is its atomic weight, which has been rounded to 75.

Elements have a property called atomic weight. The atomic weight of an element is the average weight of a typical atom of the element. All atoms of an element contain the same number of protons, but they may contain different numbers of neutrons. Because the mass of an atom is determined mostly by the number of protons and neutrons it contains, the mass of individual atoms of an element can vary from one to another. However, in the case of arsenic, all atoms found in Earth's crust are the same. Arsenic atoms contain thirty-three protons and forty-two neutrons and have a mass of 74.92 amu. Because all arsenic atoms are alike, the atomic weight of arsenic is also 74.92. In the periodic table on pages 40–41, the atomic weight for arsenic has been rounded to 75.

What Are Isotopes?

All atoms of an element have the same number of protons, but not all atoms have the same number of neutrons. Different forms of the same atom are called isotopes. The word "isotope" is Greek for "at the same place." All isotopes of an element occupy the same place on the periodic table.

The atomic mass for an element on the periodic table is an average of the atomic masses of all isotopes of the element. Naturally occurring arsenic has forty-two neutrons. However, atoms of arsenic can also have as many as fifty-nine or as few as twenty-seven neutrons. Arsenic has thirty-three isotopes, but only one of them—the one with an atomic mass of seventy-five—is stable. This is the isotope that appears in 100 percent of all natural sources of the element. The rest are man-made and radioactive.

Groups and Periods

Once Mendeleyev organized the periodic table by atomic weight, the elements were lined up in columns called groups, and rows called periods. There are eighteen groups on the periodic table. Groups of elements have the same number of electrons in their outer shells. The elements in a group often share traits. Arsenic is in group 15, or the nitrogen group. This group contains the elements, from top to bottom, nitrogen (N), phosphorus (P), arsenic, antimony (Sb), and bismuth (Bi). Group 15 elements are known for their stability in compounds because they are able to form multiple strong bonds with other elements. Group 15 elements—specifically phosphorous, arsenic, and antimony—are highly toxic.

There are seven rows, or periods, in the periodic table. All elements in the same period have the same number of electron shells, although they have different numbers of electrons in that shell. Arsenic is in period 4. All elements in period 4 have four electron shells.

What Is a Metalloid?

Nearly every chemical element on the periodic table can be identified as a metal or a nonmetal. Metals are shiny, they conduct electricity, and most are malleable—that is, they bend, not break, when hammered. Nonmetals are the opposite. They are not shiny, most do not conduct electricity, and if they are solid, they are brittle. A small group of elements exhibit some characteristics of both metals and nonmetals. These elements are sometimes called semi-metals, or metalloids. Metalloids include boron (B), silicon (Si), germanium (Ge), arsenic, antimony, tellurium (Te), and polonium (Po). The position of the metalloids on the periodic table

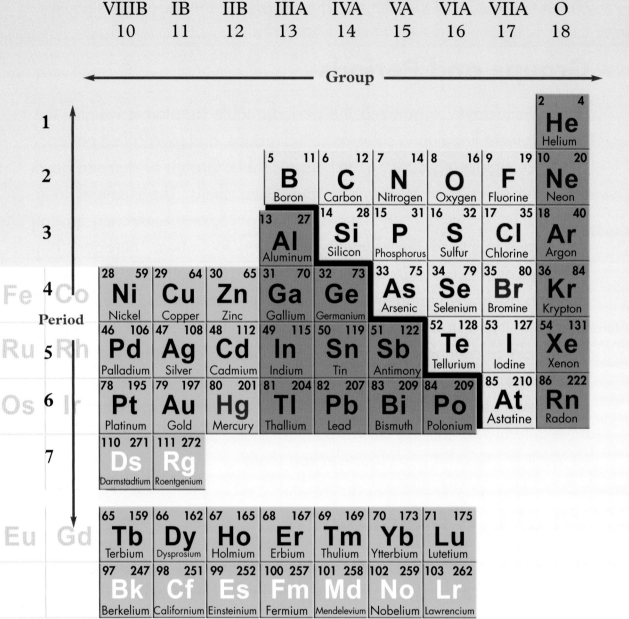

The left half of the periodic table highlights the position of the metalloids. The bold black zigzag line represents the border between the metals and nonmetals. The metalloids straddle this line. Arsenic is located in period 4 and group 15 (VA).

The arrangement of atoms in the crystal structure of solid polonium, a metalloid, has a cubic pattern, as shown in this computer model.

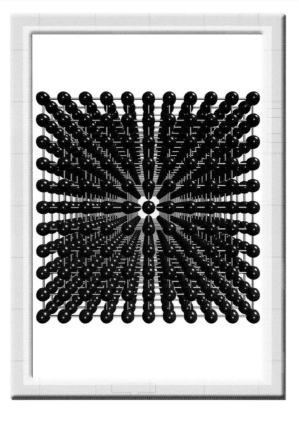

form a border between the metals and nonmetals.

At room temperature (68° Fahrenheit; 20° Celsius), metalloids are dull, brittle, and usually conduct electricity poorly. They act more like conductors at higher temperatures or when combined with other elements. This characteristic allows them to serve special purposes as semiconductors in circuits and electronic devices. Gallium arsenide (GaAs) is a compound commonly used in transistors, circuits, light emitting diodes (LEDs), and other electronic components.

There are three forms of solid arsenic: gray, yellow, and black. Scientists call different forms of an element allotropes. In allotropes, the atoms are bonded together in different patterns. Graphite and diamond are two allotropes of carbon (C). Pure arsenic is most often silver-gray with a dull luster, but it tarnishes to dark gray or black when exposed to the air. It is usually stored in a gas such as argon (Ar) in order to keep it from tarnishing. It is odorless and tasteless. It conducts heat and electricity, but not as well as copper. Pure arsenic is brittle and breaks easily.

When heated in air, arsenic oxidizes, burning with a blue flame and forming arsenic trioxide (As_2O_3). Pure arsenic is not very poisonous. However, arsenic trioxide, also called white arsenic, is very poisonous and has the odor of garlic. When gray arsenic is heated to 1,141°F (616°C), it changes directly from a solid to a gas. This process is known as sublimation. At pressures twenty-eight times atmospheric pressure, however, arsenic can be forced to melt to a liquid at 1,503°F (817°C). Arsenic is often found in sulfide ores—ores in which negatively charged sulfur ions bond to positively charged metal ions, such as iron (Fe).

Arsenic is similar to two other elements in group 15 of the periodic table: phosphorous and antimony. Phosphorous also has several allotropes, and it is very toxic. Antimony is a metalloid with several allotropic forms. It

Arsenic Snapshot

Chemical Symbol:	As
Classification:	Nonmetal, metalloid
Properties:	Brittle and silver-gray, tarnishes to black when exposed to air; a yellow form is also found in nature
Discovered By:	Albertus Magnus in 1250
Atomic Number:	33
Atomic Weight:	74.92 atomic mass units (amu)
Protons:	33
Electrons:	33
Neutrons:	42
State of Matter at 68°F (20°C):	Solid
Melting Point:	1,503°F (817°C) (at 28 times standard atmospheric pressure)
Boiling Point:	Sublimes at 1,141°F (616°C)
Commonly Found:	In Earth's crust (about 1.5–2.0 parts per million) in the minerals arsenopyrite, realgar, and orpiment

looks very similar to arsenic, is found with the same elements arsenic is found with, and even sublimes when heated. Moreover, it is difficult to tell them apart without special tests. The mineral stibarsen is a mixture of arsenic and antimony. It often takes a trained mineralogist to tell the differences among arsenic, antimony, and stibarsen.

Where Is Arsenic Found?

Arsenic is widely found in Earth's crust throughout the world but most often in low concentrations (these concentrations can be as low as 1.5 parts per million and as high as 2.1 parts per million). It is usually part of a compound, although small amounts of the pure element do exist. A small amount of arsenic enters the atmosphere when volcanoes erupt and when fossil fuels are burned. It is often found in and around hydrothermal veins along with other semi-metals. Very little arsenic is in the oceans.

Most arsenic found in nature is mixed with other substances, especially sulfides. Pure arsenic in nature is very rare. Natural crystals are often mixed with small traces of antimony, nickel (Ni), silver (Ag), iron, or sulfur (S). Pure arsenic is often contained in silver ore veins.

Arsenopyrite

The main ore of arsenic is arsenopyrite, which was once commonly called mispickle. Arsenopyrite is an iron arsenic sulfide (FeAsS) that is steel gray or silvery white. It contains about 46 percent arsenic. Arsenopyrite is often found near veins of lava and hot water. Arsenopyrite is sometimes found with gold (Au).

When arsenopyrite is exposed to the atmosphere—due to mining, construction, or natural processes—the arsenic slowly oxidizes, or joins with oxygen from the air. The arsenic oxides that form are soluble in water. The result is acidic water that can flow away from the exposed ore and pollute the nearby environment.

About two-thirds of the arsenic in Earth's atmosphere comes from man-made sources. The remaining third comes from natural sources. Most natural arsenic in the atmosphere comes from volcanic eruptions.

Realgar is arsenic sulfide. It is found in hot spring deposits and as a mineral in hydrothermal veins. The word "realgar" comes from Arabic and means "powder of the mine."

Orpiment and Realgar

Orpiment is another common ore of arsenic. It is a bright yellow sulfide of arsenic with a chemical formula of As_2S_3. It is found all over the world, often in and around openings in Earth's crust near volcanoes that emit steam and volcanic gases. The word "arsenic" originally came from the Persian word for "yellow orpiment." Another arsenic ore is realgar, a soft, orange-red mineral with a chemical formula of As_2S_2. Realgar is not as stable as orpiment, and after prolonged exposure to light, realgar can break down into a reddish yellow powder. This powder has the same chemical formula as realgar, but it has a different arrangement of atoms. Also, realgar can undergo oxidation and change into orpiment.

Orpiment and realgar were frequently traded in ancient China and Rome. They were important as pigments and medicines, despite being highly toxic. Today, orpiment is still used in the production of leather, fireworks, linoleum, and semiconductors.

Industrial Arsenic

Most industrial arsenic is obtained as a by-product from smelting ores. In 2006, the world production of arsenic was about 65,300 tons (59,200 metric tons). China is the world's top producer of arsenic; in 2006, China produced about 33,000 tons (30,000 metric tons). The United States was once a major producer of arsenic and arsenic trioxide. However, since 1968, all arsenic has been imported into the United States. Chile, Peru, Mexico, Russia, Kazakhstan, Belgium, and France are also large producers of arsenic and arsenic trioxide.

Pure arsenic is most often produced industrially by smelting iron arsenide ($FeAs_2$) or arsenopyrite to about 700°F (371°C) in the absence of air. Arsenic is obtained during the smelting of copper ores as well. This process causes the arsenic to sublime. The arsenic vapor is condensed to a solid, and then it is collected.

This photograph from 1997 shows acid mine drainage around an old silver or gold mine near the town of Ouray, Colorado. This place is one of the many acid mine drainage sites in southwest Colorado that need to be decontaminated.

When arsenic ores are heated in air (roasted), the arsenic sublimes and reacts with oxygen to form arsenic trioxide, which appears as a white smoke. This series of reactions leaves other solid oxides behind. The arsenic trioxide deposits as soot in the flue system. This process can release toxic arsenic gas into the atmosphere unless proper precautions are taken.

The Dangers of Mining

Arsenic can contaminate soil as a result of mining and smelting operations. Ores that contain arsenic are often found in the same vicinity as gold mines. Unwanted leftovers from old gold mines, called tailings, were once discarded outside the mining area. These tailings pose a health risk, especially to children who might touch the arsenic ores and then put their hands in their mouths. The leftover arsenic can also leach into the soil, making the soil unusable for farming and contaminating drinking water. Today, the tailings of mining projects are usually placed in an isolated container for future use or disposal.

Another risk associated with mining is acid mine drainage. This is a chemical reaction between water and ores that contain sulfides. The result is metal-saturated water that drains away from ore and coal mining projects. The drainage—which often contains arsenic—collects in pools and puddles not far from the mines that created them. The drainage can also pollute rivers, turning them a thick yellow, orange, or red color. Acid mine drainage can contaminate drinking water, harm plants and animals, and corrode bridges and other structures.

Chapter Four
Arsenic Compounds

A compound is a substance that contains two or more chemical elements bonded together. Atoms are able to bond together because of their electrons. The atoms in some molecules share electrons. This type of bond is called a covalent bond. Another common bond is the ionic bond. An ionic bond is one based on the attraction of opposite electrical charges. This occurs when one atom gives up electrons and becomes positively charged, or takes on (gains) electrons, becoming negatively charged.

It is the electrons in the outermost shell that form the bonds between atoms. An atom's oxidation state refers to the number of electrons an atom loses, gains, or shares when forming bonds. For example, when arsenic appears in compounds, it most commonly exists in one of three oxidation states: −3, +3, or +5. This means that it either gains three electrons from another atom, loses three electrons to another atom, or loses five electrons.

An arsenide ion is an arsenic atom with three extra electrons, and an arsenide is a compound that contains an arsenide ion. Arsenide ions have a charge of −3. An arsenate ion contains an arsenic atom bonded to four oxygen atoms and has a charge of −3. In the arsenate ion, the oxidation state of arsenic is +5. Compounds that contain these ions are also called arsenates.

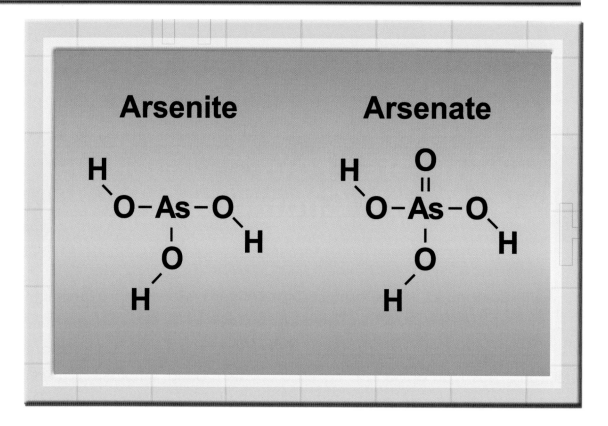

Arsenite, whose chemical formula is shown on the left, has an oxidation state of +3. It is more toxic than arsenate, whose chemical formula is shown on the right, and it is highly soluble in water. As a result, arsenite can easily contaminate groundwater.

Arsenic Oxides

An oxide is a chemical compound that contains oxygen and one other element. Most of Earth's crust is made up of oxides. They often form when elements and compounds come into contact with air. Oxides sometimes form on the surfaces of elements and compounds. Rust, for example, is a coating of iron oxide on the surface of iron objects.

Arsenic oxidizes to arsenic trioxide (As_2O_3) when heated in air. The product is also called arsenic(III) oxide and white arsenic. It is a white crystal. Arsenic trioxide is the most widely used commercial compound of arsenic. It is employed in pesticides, cancer medications, and wood

Organic or Inorganic?

Arsenic can be categorized as organic or inorganic. Inorganic arsenic—the more abundant of the two—is encountered widely in nature. Inorganic arsenic bonds to a wide variety of elements in igneous and sedimentary rocks. It is most often found bonded to sulfur, oxygen (O), and chlorine (Cl). Most inorganic arsenic compounds are white, odorless powders.

Organic arsenic compounds contain carbon and hydrogen. There is a large number of organic arsenic compounds, and they are much less poisonous than inorganic arsenic compounds. They usually smell like garlic. Organic arsenic can be created by artificial processes. However, inorganic arsenic joins with carbon and hydrogen when it enters the body to form organic arsenic. Sea animals also contain low levels of organic arsenic. Organic and inorganic arsenic can change forms, but arsenic itself can never be destroyed.

preservatives, among many other uses. Another important arsenic oxide with similar applications is arsenic(V) oxide (As_2O_5)—which is also called arsenic pentoxide.

Arsenic Hydrides

A hydride is a compound that contains hydrogen and another element. Arsenic(III) hydride (AsH_3), also known as arsine, is a colorless gas that smells like garlic. It is highly poisonous. It is also flammable and can explode unexpectedly when it comes into contact with oxidizing agents, such as oxygen. It can even explode when a mixture with oxygen is exposed to light. Arsine forms when arsenic comes into contact with an

A hazardous materials response unit in New Mexico washes off a member of the unit after inspecting a tractor trailer that leaked a herbicide containing arsenic. This herbicide can react with the aluminum of the tractor trailer to produce dangerous arsine gas.

acid. The Marsh test verifies the presence of arsenic because the arsenic in a sample reacts with zinc and sulfuric acid to produce arsine gas. Arsine was developed for use as a weapon during World War II, but it was never used. Today, arsine is used in the electronics industry in the production of semiconductors. Arsenic(II) hydride (As_2H_4) is an unstable liquid. It is sometimes called diarsine.

Arsenic Sulfides

A sulfide is a compound that contains sulfur ions, which have a −2 electrical charge. Arsenic bonds with sulfides to form many compounds. Realgar and orpiment are arsenic sulfides that are found in nature. Arsenic sulfides are generally stable at room temperature, but they can react with oxygen at higher temperatures. The human body contains sulfide ions, to which arsenic atoms easily bond.

Halogens and Arsenic Halides

Halogens make up group 17 of the periodic table. The halogens are fluorine (F), chlorine, bromine (Br), iodine (I), and astatine (At). These elements are highly reactive and are found in nature only in compounds or as negative ions. The outer electron shell of all halogens has seven electrons, which means it is one electron short of being full. Halogens tend to fill that outer shell by accepting an electron from another element. Filling the outer shell gives them an overall negative electrical charge. When combined with metals, halogens make salts. Halides are binary compounds formed by halogens. Arsenic forms many halides, all of which are highly poisonous.

Lead Arsenate

Lead arsenate ($PbHAsO_4$) was first used as a pesticide in the early 1890s. It was effective at controlling weevils, moths, grasshoppers, and other insects. Lead arsenate was

In this photograph from 1938, a man is spraying an arsenic herbicide on a putting green in Margate, England. Most agricultural uses of arsenic herbicides and pesticides are now banned.

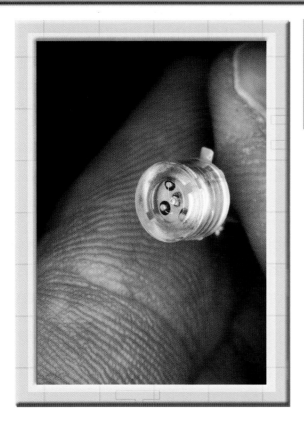

This is a gallium arsenide LED. Because of its ability to conduct electricity, gallium arsenide is frequently used as a semiconductor in electronic devices.

used well into the twentieth century on cotton farms and in fruit orchards. As with other pesticides that contain arsenic, it is now believed that lead arsenate caused cancer in workers who sprayed the chemical on plants and who inhaled the ash from waste material burned after harvest.

Gallium Arsenide

Gallium is a brittle, silvery metal that liquefies easily. In fact, it melts when held in the hand. The compound gallium arsenide (GaAs) is a popular semiconductor used in many electronic devices. Circuits made from gallium arsenide are faster but more expensive than those made from silicon (Si). You probably have several products that contain gallium arsenide in your home.

One reason gallium arsenide is so useful is because it can turn electricity into light. This function is used to create light emitting diodes (LEDs). An LED is a semiconductor that emits light when an electrical current is passed through it. It is often used as an indicator on electrical equipment. LEDs made with gallium arsenide produce a red or infrared light. Gallium arsenide was the first compound used in the commercial manufacture of LEDs in the 1960s. Since then, other compounds have been developed that create other colors.

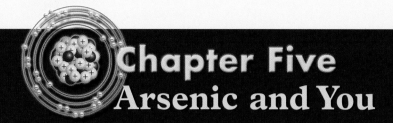

Chapter Five
Arsenic and You

In many cases, just 100 milligrams of arsenic is enough to kill a human being. Inorganic arsenic is more toxic than organic arsenic. Ingesting and inhaling arsenic is far more dangerous than simply touching it. Arsenic poisoning can be difficult to diagnose because most of it leaves the body within three days of exposure. The rest is stored in the brain, bones, and some tissues.

Arsenic binds to sulfides in the body and inhibits enzymes in the digestive system. This action disrupts the body's processes of metabolism. Acute arsenic poisoning results in widespread organ failure. The symptoms resemble those of cholera. They include severe stomach pains, vomiting, diarrhea, internal bleeding, shivering, headaches, delirium, coma, heart failure, and death. The symptoms of chronic poisoning include white lines spanning the fingernails and toenails, discoloration of the skin, warts and bumps, and gangrene. These symptoms can appear as early as two weeks, or may not appear for years. Long-term symptoms can include cancer, heart disease, and diabetes.

Drinking Water in Bangladesh

In the 1970s, surface water in Bangladesh became too polluted to drink. Thousands of wells were dug to access groundwater. Today, there are

Clean drinking water in Bangladesh is very hard to come by. The situation is made more dire by well water contaminated with arsenic. People who live in a poverty-stricken area are seen here using swamp water for their daily cleaning.

more than 11,000,000 wells in the country, approximately 90 percent of which are believed to be contaminated with arsenic. The acceptable arsenic limit designated by the World Health Organization (WHO) is 10 parts per billion (ppb). Nearly half of the wells tested have arsenic levels higher than 50 ppb. These arsenic levels have led to the worst case of mass poisoning in history.

A number of solutions have been suggested and implemented. Some people purify their water as it is taken from the well, although this may not always be effective. Some have dug deeper wells, which tap into water that is uncontaminated or less contaminated. Others have water delivered. Still others collect rainwater. Scientists believe these systems are improving the situation in Bangladesh, but constant monitoring and testing is required to be sure.

What Is CCA?

Chromated copper arsenate (CCA) has been used since the 1940s as a wood preservative. Since the 1970s, most of the wood used to build playground equipment, picnic tables, patios, and landscaping structures in the United States have been made with CCA-treated wood. The copper protects the wood against decay caused by fungi and bacteria. The arsenic protects wood against insects. The chromium (Cr) binds the other chemicals to wood fibers. The CCA gives wood a green tint.

Studies conducted in the 1980s revealed that chromium does not bind the other chemicals to wood fibers as well as it was originally believed to. In many cases, the chromium, copper, and arsenic slowly leached into the ground around structures, contaminating the soil. The poison can rub off on hands and can enter the body when children put their hands in their mouths. Sawdust produced when cutting CCA-treated wood is dangerous when inhaled. Once these results were publicized, people began tearing down playgrounds and other structures made with

CCA-treated wood. Much of this wood was burned, which released poisonous arsenic ash into the atmosphere. This toxic pollution continues to be a problem today.

As of December 30, 2003—thanks to steps taken by the U.S. Environmental Protection Agency (EPA)—CCA-treated wood is no longer used in the construction of most residential structures, including play sets and patios. This action was designed to reduce the chances of accidental arsenic poisoning, especially to children. Other countries around the world followed suit. The chemical is still used in instances when contact with humans and animals is unlikely.

Insects, Rodents, Fungi, Weeds, and . . . Chickens?

Arsenic has been used as a pesticide for many years. Lead arsenate was used in apple orchards from the 1800s until the 1940s. This use resulted in soil contaminated with lead and arsenic. It also caused many farm workers to become sick and develop cancer. The chemical monosodium methyl arsenate (MSMA), which hit the market in the 1960s, is a popular herbicide used on golf courses and cotton farms. Once again, high arsenic levels of arsenic in the soil have led to it being used less and less. However, MSMA and other inorganic arsenic pesticides are still used in the United States.

Although arsenic is poisonous to people, it is a trace element for some animals, including rats, pigs, shrimp, oysters, and algae. Without arsenic, chickens will not grow as large as they would with the element. Arsenic has been a government-approved additive in chicken feed for decades. It helps kill parasites and improves growth. Many scientists, however, insist that it is unnecessary. Some chicken farmers have stopped feeding it to their chickens, although most still do.

Arsenic as a Medicine

People typically ingest as much as 1 milligram of arsenic in their daily diet, but this is too low to cause any harm. It is usually excreted from the body in the urine. Some scientists think arsenic might be a trace element for people, but no one is sure how it works in the body. It does act as a stimulant and boosts the formation of red blood cells. Historically, medications that contained arsenic had been prescribed for a number of ailments, including malaria, diabetes, and tuberculosis. Many of these "medications" have been proven to be ineffective, unnecessary, or deadly.

Despite its dangers, there are medical uses for arsenic today. Drugs made with arsenic are called arsenicals. The drug carbarsone is sometimes used to treat dysentery. The drug Trisenox, which contains arsenic trioxide, is sometimes used to treat leukemia. It increases the number of healthy blood cells that have been diminished by cancerous white blood cells. Although research into the effectiveness of Trisenox is ongoing, studies show that it is often successful in achieving complete or temporary remission.

Semiconductors

A semiconductor is a substance that conducts electricity better than an insulator—such as rubber or glass—but not as well as a conductor—such as copper. This quality makes semiconductors more effective than conductors in some electronics because they are able to limit the amount of electricity flowing through a device. Most of the metalloids are used as semiconductors, particularly silicon. Semiconductors are an important component of modern devices that contain transistors. These include radios, televisions, computers, lasers, cell phones, and the solar cells that provide power to man-made satellites.

Two scientists at Motorola Labs, Dr. Jamal Ramdani (left) and Dr. Ravi Droopad, hold the first twelve-inch gallium arsenide and silicon wafer in 2001. As a semi-conductor, the GaAs-on-silicon wafer has made electronics cheaper, faster, and more effective than some other semiconductors.

Gallium arsenide is commonly used in semiconductors today. Indium-gallium-arsenide is used to make some of the fastest electronics at present. It is also used to make machines that detect infrared light. Other arsenic compounds that are used as semiconductors include aluminum arsenide (AlAs), cadmium arsenide (Cd_3As_2), and indium arsenide (InAs).

Living with Arsenic

The use of arsenic in society has dwindled over the years because of its toxicity. However, it is still used in specialized industries. It is used to decolorize glass and to make car batteries. It is alloyed with metals such as lead to make them stronger at higher temperatures. Scientists today know more about arsenic than ever before. Although this has certainly reduced the extent of its usefulness in society, it has also pinpointed the areas where it can best be used to serve humanity. Knowing more about arsenic has also led to fewer cases of arsenic poisoning and pollution in the world. People who work with arsenic now know the importance of wearing coveralls, gloves, glasses, and respirators. Further study is ongoing and will help to improve the lives of people subjected to arsenic poisoning, especially the people of Bangladesh.

The Periodic Table of Elements

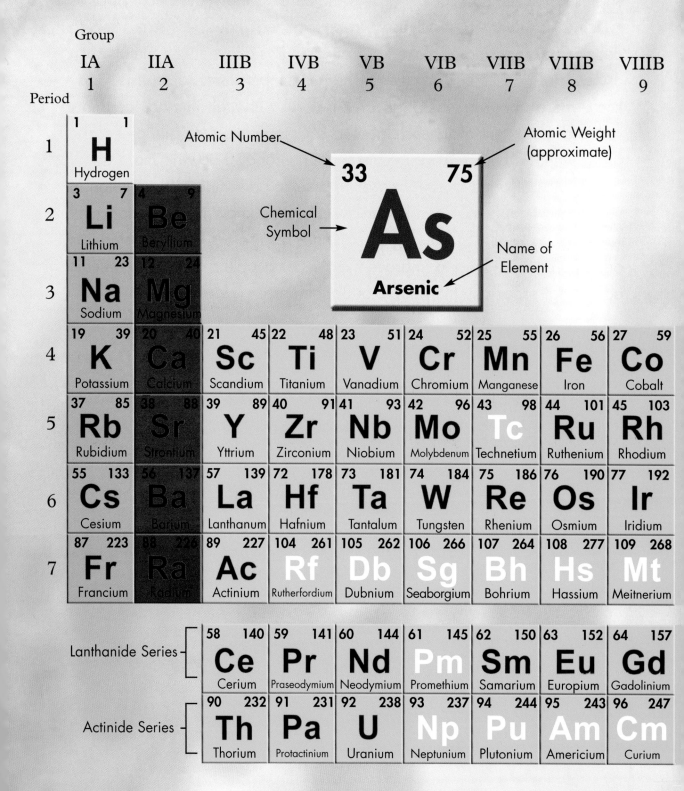

Group

	IA	IIA	IIIB	IVB	VB	VIB	VIIB	VIIIB	VIIIB
	1	2	3	4	5	6	7	8	9

Atomic Number

Atomic Weight (approximate)

Chemical Symbol

Name of Element

33		75
	As	
	Arsenic	

Period

1	1 H Hydrogen								
2	3 Li 7 Lithium	4 Be 9 Beryllium							
3	11 Na 23 Sodium	12 Mg 24 Magnesium							
4	19 K 39 Potassium	20 Ca 40 Calcium	21 Sc 45 Scandium	22 Ti 48 Titanium	23 V 51 Vanadium	24 Cr 52 Chromium	25 Mn 55 Manganese	26 Fe 56 Iron	27 Co 59 Cobalt
5	37 Rb 85 Rubidium	38 Sr 88 Strontium	39 Y 89 Yttrium	40 Zr 91 Zirconium	41 Nb 93 Niobium	42 Mo 96 Molybdenum	43 Tc 98 Technetium	44 Ru 101 Ruthenium	45 Rh 103 Rhodium
6	55 Cs 133 Cesium	56 Ba 137 Barium	57 La 139 Lanthanum	72 Hf 178 Hafnium	73 Ta 181 Tantalum	74 W 184 Tungsten	75 Re 186 Rhenium	76 Os 190 Osmium	77 Ir 192 Iridium
7	87 Fr 223 Francium	88 Ra 226 Radium	89 Ac 227 Actinium	104 Rf 261 Rutherfordium	105 Db 262 Dubnium	106 Sg 266 Seaborgium	107 Bh 264 Bohrium	108 Hs 277 Hassium	109 Mt 268 Meitnerium

Lanthanide Series

58 Ce 140 Cerium	59 Pr 141 Praseodymium	60 Nd 144 Neodymium	61 Pm 145 Promethium	62 Sm 150 Samarium	63 Eu 152 Europium	64 Gd 157 Gadolinium

Actinide Series

90 Th 232 Thorium	91 Pa 231 Protactinium	92 U 238 Uranium	93 Np 237 Neptunium	94 Pu 244 Plutonium	95 Am 243 Americium	96 Cm 247 Curium

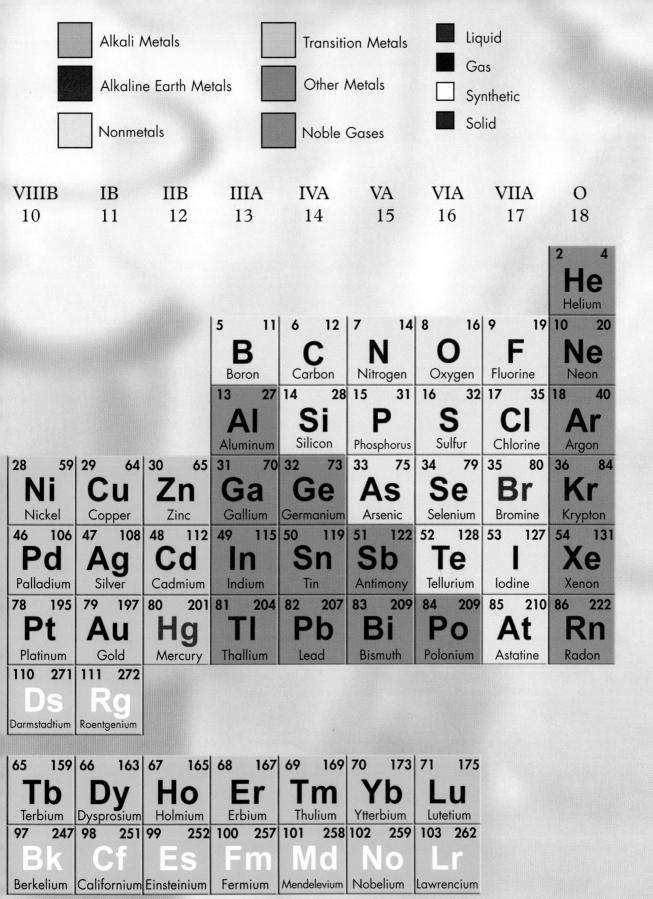

Glossary

acute Describing an illness that has a rapid onset and a severe outcome.

binary compound A chemical compound that contains two chemical elements.

cholera An illness, potentially fatal, caused by water or food contaminated with bacteria.

chronic Describing an illness that lasts over a long period and often causes long-term changes in the body.

delirium A state marked by fever, restlessness, confusion, and sometimes hallucinations.

dysentery A disease of the lower intestines marked by severe diarrhea and caused by bacteria or other parasites.

enzyme A complex protein made by cells that helps control a chemical reaction in the body. There are many different enzymes.

gangrene The death and decay of tissues of the body due to a lack of blood to that area.

hydrothermal Relating to hot water in or on Earth's crust.

leach To dissolve in rainwater and pass into the soil.

leukemia A cancer that causes white blood cells to take the place of red blood cells.

oxide A compound that contains oxygen combined with another element, especially a metal.

pigment A solid substance added to give something a color.

radioactive Referring to a substance that emits energy in the form of a stream of subatomic particles and energy as it decays.

smelting To melt ore in order to separate metal from it.

soluble Able to be dissolved in another substance.

theologian An expert or student of theology, the study of religion.

American Chemical Society
1155 Sixteenth Street NW
Washington, DC 20036
(800) 227-5558 (U.S. only); (202) 872-4600 (outside the U.S.)
Web site: http://www.chemistry.org
This organization provides news, information, and resources for chemists. Members receive extra benefits, such as career services, networking opportunities, and free subscriptions to industry magazines.

Centers for Disease Control and Prevention (CDC)
1600 Clifton Road
Atlanta, GA 30333
(404) 639-3534
Web site: http://www.cdc.gov
The CDC's mission is to "to promote health and quality of life by preventing and controlling disease, injury, and disability."

U.S. Environmental Protection Agency (EPA)
Ariel Rios Building
1200 Pennsylvania Avenue NW
Washington, DC 20460
(202) 272-0167
Web site: http://www.epa.gov
This organization is dedicated to protecting the environment and human health. It develops and enforces regulations regarding environmental laws, performs environmental research, and promotes education about the environment.

World Health Organization (WHO)
Avenue Appia 20
CH - 1211 Geneva 27
Switzerland
+41 22 791 2111
Web site: http://www.who.int/en
Backed by the United Nations, WHO provides leadership on global
    health matters. It works to strengthen health systems, conducts
    research, and improves the health of communities all over the world.

Web Sites

Due to the changing nature of Internet links, Rosen Publishing has
developed an online list of Web sites related to the subject of this book.
This site is updated regularly. Please use this link to access the list:

http://www.rosenlinks.com/uept/arsn

For Further Reading

Cooper, Chris. *Arsenic*. New York, NY: Benchmark Books, 2006.

Miller, Ron. *The Elements: What You Really Want to Know*. Minneapolis, MN: Twenty-First Century Books, 2006.

Newmark, Ann, and Laura Buller. *Chemistry*. New York, NY: DK Children, 2005.

Oxlade, Chris. *Elements and Compounds* (Chemicals in Action). Chicago, IL: Heinemann Library, 2002.

Parker, Steve. *Rocks and Minerals*. New York, NY: DK Children, 1997.

Pough, Frederick H. *Peterson First Guide to Rocks and Minerals*. New York, NY: Houghton Mifflin, 1991.

Stwertka, Albert. *A Guide to the Elements*. 2nd ed. New York, NY: Oxford University Press, 2002.

Tweed, Matt. *Essential Elements: Atoms, Quarks, and the Periodic Table*. New York, NY: Walker, 2003.

Zannos, Susan. *Dmitri Mendeleyev and the Periodic Table* (Uncharted, Unexplored, and Unexplained). Hockessin, DE: Mitchell Lane Publishers, 2004.

Bibliography

Brooks, William E. "Arsenic." U.S. Geological Survey, Mineral Commodity Summaries, January 2007. Retrieved September 25, 2007 (http://minerals.usgs.gov/minerals/pubs/commodity/arsenic/arsenmcs07.pdf).

Committee of Medical and Biological Effects of Environmental Pollutants. *Arsenic.* Washington, D.C.: National Academies Press, 1977.

Emsley, John. *Nature's Building Blocks: An A–Z Guide to the Elements.* Oxford, England: Oxford University Press, 2001.

Greenwood, N. N., and A. Earnshaw. *Chemistry of the Elements.* Oxford, England: Butterworth-Heinemann, 2001.

Kevles, Daniel J. "Don't Chew the Wallpaper: A History of Poison." Slate.com, April 6, 2006. Retrieved September 11, 2007 (http://www.slate.com/id/2139414).

Krebs, Robert E. *The History and Use of Our Earth's Chemical Elements: A Reference Guide.* Westport, CT: Greenwood Press, 1998.

Scheindlin, Stanley. "The Duplicitous Nature of Inorganic Arsenic." Molecular Inventions. Retrieved September 6, 2007 (http://molinterv.aspetjournals.org/cgi/content/full/5/2/60).

Smith, Roger. "Arsenic: A Murderous History." Dartmouth Toxic Metals Research Program, July 26, 2002. Retrieved September 11, 2007 (http://www.dartmouth.edu/~toxmetal/TXSHas.htm).

United States Geological Survey. "Mine Drainage." Geology in the Eastern Region. Retrieved September 24, 2007 (http://geology.er.usgs.gov/eastern/environment/drainage.html).

Wilson, Richard. "Chronic Arsenic Poisoning: History, Study and Remediation." Harvard Physics Department, July 12, 2007. Retrieved September 12, 2007 (http://www.physics.harvard.edu/~wilson/arsenic/arsenic_project_introduction.html).

Index

About the Author

Greg Roza has written and edited educational materials for children and young adults for the past eight years. He has a master's degree in English from the State University of New York at Fredonia. Roza has long had an interest in scientific topics, including chemistry, and spends much of his spare time tinkering with machines around the house. He lives in Hamburg, New York, with his wife, Abigail, and his three children, Autumn, Lincoln, and Daisy.

Photo Credits

Cover, pp. 1, 14, 40–41 Tahara Anderson; p. 5 © G. DeGrazia/Custom Medical Stock Photo; p. 6 © Christian Hartmann/epa/Corbis; p. 8 © dpa/Corbis; p. 9 © Metropolitan Museum of Art/Art Resource, NY; p. 10 © Scala/Art Resource; p. 13 Lester V. Bergmman/Corbis; p. 19 © Dr. Mark J. Winter/SPL/Photo Researchers, Inc.; pp. 23, 34 © AFP/ Getty Images; p. 24 © Weinstein/Custom Medical Stock Photo; p. 25 © Aurora/Getty Images; pp. 30, 38 © AP Photos; p. 31 © Getty Images; p. 32 © Mike McNamee/Photo Researchers, Inc.

Designer: Tahara Anderson; **Editor:** Kathy Kuhtz Campbell
Photo Researcher: Marty Levick